T0113914

THE
JOURNEY

POEMS OF SALVATION

Regina Marie Blaylock

WESTBOW
PRESS®
A DIVISION OF THOMAS NELSON
& ZONDERVAN

WestBow Press books may be ordered through booksellers or by contacting:

WestBow Press
A Division of Thomas Nelson & Zondervan
1663 Liberty Drive
Bloomington, IN 47403
www.westbowpress.com
844-714-3454

Scripture taken from the King James Version of the Bible.

ISBN: 978-1-6642-5455-8 (sc)
ISBN: 978-1-6642-5454-1 (hc)
ISBN: 978-1-6642-5456-5 (e)

Library of Congress Control Number: 2022901820

Print information available on the last page.

WestBow Press rev. date: 01/29/2022

I dedicate this collection of poems to my father, Clifford A. Husereau. He spent his life working hard and persevering through difficult times. He provided for me and my six siblings. He changed dramatically when my eldest brother was dying of cancer at a young age. I saw him go from dark hair to gray hair in a matter of months due to worry. One thing he taught me that I have never forgotten is that God is who you turn to when you are alone and troubled. God will get you through. He gave me a gift I will always cherish because God is who has gotten me through my many trials.

He is the reason I stand strong today.

Introduction

This collection of poems I have written over many years. "A Beacon in the Night" was one of the first poems I wrote. God is guiding my life now. But this doesn't mean there won't be difficult times. In March 2015 I lost our home. My children and I were separated. We were reunited in January 2016. We are healing and getting back on our feet again. God has brought us many blessings in the storm. God is shaping and guiding me. During this time of silence and healing he has given me many beautiful poems, many of which have answered questions and confusions about my life and his will for me. He has revealed the imposters and the truths. He is helping me stand stronger. Sometimes we are the ones who must face personal truths to help us grow and learn. I wrote "Domestic Abuse" in the acceptance of that is what my marriage was.

In my journey with God, he has shown me deep compassion and love. When I am fearful or tearing myself down, he picks me up and shows me my beauty and his will for me. He gave me "Whispers" during one of those times. I want others to know how beautiful the love of God is. We don't have to control things or carry the burdens. Some things are only for God to do.

God has been taking his time revealing the truths in my life and healing me. He has been justifying me to others who have spread vile gossip. He has been walking patiently and picked me up every time I have fallen. He has shown me through these trials I am stronger and closer to him. He has also shown me how he has used my life to make changes in the people around me who have judged me. He is changing things for the good of all. This book ends with "Salvation" because God has saved my life and the lives of my children from those who have meant us great harm. He has drawn us closer to him.

I hope these poems touch your heart, no matter where you are on your journey with God.

Contents

CHAPTER 1
Out of the Ashes

I wrote "Domestic Abuse" about my first marriage. I struggled against much betrayal and hidden truths. It took a long time because God knew my heart. He knew I couldn't take all the truths at once. Many of them were heart-wrenching. I have finally come to call it what it was—domestic abuse.

I wrote "The Shunning" after being shunned by many people, including the people at my church. After losing my home and trying to get back up on my feet, I posted a flyer about a book signing on the church bulletin board. Someone from my church ripped it down. No one came to the book signing.

I wrote "My Friend" about the time during the shunning when no one would speak to me because of much gossip and untruths. A friend was shopping at the grocery store near me and never acknowledged me. It was very hurtful.

I wrote "Where Are the Bluebirds?" after we lost our home. When I got a divorce and my life was starting over, there were bluebirds flying around in our subdivision. To me, they were a symbol from God that he was here, and we were safe. When we lost our home, I kept looking for the bluebirds.

"A Grieving Mother" is a poem of compassion about a mother whom I helped with her child. Sometimes the babies I work with die. But I work with families as well as their children. To me, it is humbling to remember them because they shared their most precious gift with me.

I had to write "This Is Me." When you are a victim of domestic abuse, you are surviving and trying to keep the ship steady against much sabotage. You stay quiet. "This Is Me" is about who I am. No one really knew me, Gina.

"I Sit … I Watch …" is about the numbness that you feel when all is lost and the fear you have when attempting to stand up, try again, and trust again. Only God could help me do this.

> "Lord who shall abide in thy tabernacle? Who shall dwell in thy holy hill? He that walketh uprightly, and worketh righteousness, and speaketh the truth in his heart." (Psalm 15:1–2 KJV)

Domestic Abuse

I walked into the
Ladies' room at my church.
There were cards on the vanity
For women of domestic abuse.
I thought, *I can't pick this up.*
No one would believe me.
No one knows my pain.
They will chastise my children.
We will be put to shame.
So, I washed my hands and left.
I joined the service of prayer.
God knows my heart.
He knows my despair.
I walked into the bathroom.
A card was on the vanity,
A helpline number
For women of domestic abuse,
But I could not pick it up.
They would never believe me.
My children would pay the price.
They don't know the same
Person I do;
He seems so nice.
I carry a heavy burden.
No one can know the truth
For my children would pay the price.
I must endure this abuse.
I came home from my
Marathon training
To take my children shopping.
My husband cursed at me and
Spit on me in front of them.
This was the end,
The final chapter.
For everything I endured,

He was careful not to let
Them see.
But today I was nothing,
And my children got to see.
I filed for divorce.
I stayed in our home.
I endured much abuse
During those long months.
But when I stood in the
Courthouse,
He pleaded with the judge.
He loved me and would
Marry me again.
But this was not love!
I stood up strong and
Opened my mouth;
I said my final words:
"I do not want this
Marriage;
I would never go back
To him."
I left the courthouse,
And when I reached my truck,
A dozen red roses were inside,
But it was still locked!
He approached me,
But I stood firm.
I drove away free that day,
Happy my children were with me
And that their futures would be
Bright and gay.
But the days, weeks, and months
To follow
Were not as pleasant as they seemed.
My phone was tampered with—
Calls from his friends making inquiries,
Hang-up calls,
Calls of threats filled the days.

I kept quiet.
I didn't want my children
To live in fear.
I stood up strong
To my abuser,
But my family and friends,
They did not see the same
For I was so careful
About hiding all my pain,
And whenever they get the chance
They remember him by name.
But now my abuser
Has passed on.
Many glorify his name.
Why don't women
Speak about their abusers?
They will be put to shame.
Gossip and lies will surround them.
Their children will endure the pain.
No one was there
When the abuse was happening.
No one lived what I lived.
But they judge and chastise me.
They try to put me to shame.
My Father above
Loves me.
He helped me heal the pain.
He showed me the beauty inside me.
He has healed all my pain.
Why do women endure such abuse?
Because
No one
     Is
         Listening!
They do not want to
           Know
             The
               Truth!

The Shunning

They shunned me
When my children
Were happy.
They were jealous.
They shunned me when my children
Lost their father.
They were righteous.
They shunned me
When I stood up
For my family.
They thought
I shouldn't have fought.
They shunned me when I couldn't stand
And carry their weight
Of chastisement.
They were happy.
They were satisfied.
They shunned me
When I helped them.
They didn't accept me
In their club.
They shunned me
When I thanked them
For helping me with
Children's ministry.
They felt justified.
They shunned me
When I tried to
Stand up on my feet.
Their eyes were cold.
Their backs were turned.
They shunned me
When I stood up and
Began to care for
My children again.

They smiled fake smiles,
Made empty gestures,
But never befriended me.
They shunned me when
I gave them gifts.
They wanted me to go.
Their shunning
Was based on
Gossip and lies,
And when I fell,
Their shunning was
Justified.
They grew hatred;
I gave love.
They grew despisement;
I gave friendship.
They grew colder;
I gave gifts.
I can't satisfy them;
They have asked me
To leave.
They feel I am evil.
They feel I reap
What I sow.
They are a club.
They pat one another
On the back.
They stand up and
Speak loudly
About their good deeds,
But God's hand
Is on me.
He has silenced me.
He has taught me
Humility.
He has strengthened me,
Caressed and consoled me
In my darkest hour.

They throw stones,
But God won't let them
Bruise me.
He wraps me in
His armor.
He shields me from
The pain they inflict.
He tells me
He loves me,
And this too
Shall pass.
But the shunning
Continues,
And I pray for him
To protect me and
Watch over my family.
He says,
"It's almost over."
He says,
"Joy will be here again,
Great joy!"
For now,
This is the shunning,
And my Lord
He is protecting me.
He is revealing truths
And justifying me.
I pray to him.
I ask for
The shunning to stop!

My Friend

My friend,
I saw you today.
My friend from long ago,
You were shopping near me,
But you did not say
Hello.
I saw you today
Looking quiet and content.
You noticed me
But did not say a word.
We used to walk together
And talk nonstop.
We shared our joys and worries.
We talked about our families.
You were my friend.
You needed help.
I was there.
You were struggling and
God sent me to
Cheer you up.
I gave you a figurine of
The bluebird of happiness
To let you know I cared.
But today I walked
Quietly throughout the store,
Asking God
Why you did not say
Hello!
You used to be my friend.
I never judged you.
I helped you in times
Of trouble.
But today,
Silence.
You did not say hello!

Where Are the Bluebirds?

One day I stood up and
Stood up strong against
My oppressor.
God helped me lift my head.
He taught me how
Beautiful I really am.
He took me on a journey
To a new place.
He brought friendly people
Around me.
He brought the bluebirds
All around me.
I would see them
When I walked in the evening.
He would always bring my
Attention to them.
Some days the bluebirds would
Fly ahead of me
To the tree in my front yard.
In the rainstorms,
He would stop me
In my tracks
And alert me to the
Sun appearing as he painted
A rainbow across the sky.
He brought my first friend
In this new place
With a gift of violets
In a shoe with a bluebird on top.
She became a good friend.
Our families grew to
Know one another.
She helped me when we were
In a time of sadness.
But one day

The rainbows and bluebirds
Disappeared.
Our new home
Was gone.
So were my new friends.
Now I am in a small place
(That is what they call it when
You no longer have a house.)
It hurts and I have struggled,
Searching for the bluebirds.
My daughter rescued a crow
With a hurt wing,
But no bluebirds.
I walk quietly from time to time,
But this is not the country road
I am used to walking.
People seem nice here.
God is here helping us
In the times when we cannot stand.
Now he is showing me
Hope for a future
For my daughter and me.
We want a *home*.
For now, each day
I look outside for the
Bluebirds.
We were so happy!
It's hard to understand
The times that have brought
Us here.
I ask God,
"Where are the bluebirds?"

You Came into My Life

You came into my life
Full of joy,
Full of gifts of love.
You came into my life
Without a care in the world.
You were so innocent,
You gave me much
Compassion.
You were so small,
Your eyes lit up a room
As if every day were a party!
You came into my life.
Everything in your life
Was a struggle …
… to breathe
… to play
… to crawl
… to walk
But you met each challenge
With such enormous strength.
You came into my life.
We laughed,
We played,
You hugged,
You were determined to learn.
WOW!
What a joy you were.
We sang,
You played the drums.
You stepped up to
That walker
And pushed it with ease.
You paused and looked at me,
Your smile was exuberant.
You held the walker

With one hand,
Then you walked away
From it with such confidence.
We all clapped
And you were overjoyed.
Throughout it all,
You had your falls.
You were rushed off
To the hospital.
Battle after battle,
Each time you came back
Like a champ.
You came into my life,
You warmed my heart,
You touched my soul.
And when the angels came
To take you home,
You stayed in my heart.
You have touched my soul
Forever.
I see you every day
A new baby smiles at me.
You came into my life.
You were
Joy, love and grace.
You came into my life.
Though you are with the angels now,
Every day you are with me,
In my heart and in my soul.
You came into my life,
You are engraved on my soul.
You came into my life.
Every day you touched me.
Thank you …
You were love!

A Grieving Mother

(The loss of a baby)
Today I looked up,
You walked by my classroom,
Pausing only for a moment.
I felt your heart hurting,
Your look of loss and of love.
You wanted me to know
You were grateful,
Your precious angel
Has gone home to the Lord,
He is taking care of her.
Today our eyes met,
Our hearts met.
Not as teacher and parent
But as Mother's who love.
Today I felt your loss,
I felt your appreciation,
I felt your love.
Not a word did you say.
I hope you come back,
I know it is hard.
Your angel is in heaven,
But you and I our hearts met
And we both love your angel.
I wish you peace,
For God has a purpose
In all things
That we cannot just yet understand.
I hope you come back,
For God brought us together
For a reason.

If I Have Love

If I have Love …
        … I have everything
I have happiness
        … security
        … warmth
        … endearment
        … Great Joy!
If I have Love …
        … I have everything
I have kisses & hugs
        … serenity
        … calm
        … balance
        … spontaneity
If I have Love …
        … I have everything
I have cherished memories
        … times turning
        … unexpected surprises
        … joyful laughter
        … holidays
        … family & friends
If I have Love …
        … I have everything
I have compassion
        … hearts locking
        … never letting go
        … a compelling urge to rescue
        … random acts of kindness
        … many blessings
If I have Love …
… I have everything
I have Grace …
        … Forgiveness
        … Protection from God's Angels

... Strength beyond the power of man
... Blessings
Too many to
Count!
If I have Love ...
I have everything ...
My Creator meant for me to have ...
I have ...
LIFE!

You Came!

You came
But you didn't stay.
I prayed.
You came, you played,
But you didn't stay.
I prayed.
You came, you cried,
But you didn't stay.
I prayed.
You came, you tried,
But you couldn't change.
You didn't stay.
I prayed.
You came, you turned me away,
You didn't stay.
I prayed.
You came, you opened your heart,
You said I was your sweetheart,
But you didn't stay.
I prayed.
You came, you said,
I'll be OK,
But you didn't stay.
I prayed.
You came to tell me
You would pray for me,
I knew you were on your way,
You didn't stay.
I prayed.
You had loss,
I prayed.
You disappeared,
I prayed.
"God, please bring him
       To stay …
              … someday!

I Sit ... I Watch ...

I sit ... I watch ...
They come; they go ...
I sit ... They fly ...
They sing ... They laugh ...
I sit ... They are off again
On a new adventure ...
I sit ... quiet ... watching ...
They come; they go ...
Now there is snow ...
I sit ... I watch ... in the quiet ...
They play, they joke and tease ...
The laughter is life.
They celebrate it.
I sit ... I watch ...
I'm afraid ...
For I have been terribly hurt.
I pray, I draw, I write
They come; they go ...
Playing in the snow.
I sit ... quiet ... never stirring.
I'm afraid ... to live ...
For gossip has imprisoned me
They come; they go ...
They don't know ...
I sit ... I cry ...
I pray ... I try ...
They come; they go ...
My how they've grown
I sit ...
Watching it all pass me by
I want to try ... I cry ...
I pray ... I stand ...
He lifts me up ...
He carries me ...
I can walk ...

I can run …
I can stand out
In the sun
I pray …
I thank him in song
They come … They stay …
We pray …
We love … We play …
He comes … to take me away …
They come … They pray …
They say …
They will see me …
Someday!

This is Me!

I am alive! I am kind!
This is me you will find.
I play, I laugh,
I like to stay out
In the sun.
I dress up pretty,
I fix my hair;
Sometimes I just put on
My walking shoes.
This is Me!
I like to walk,
I like to run
Out in the sun,
On a country road,
With the colorful leaves
And the cool breeze.
I love to stop and
Listen to the birds.
This is Me!
I love the beach,
To play and swim
In the water,
To sail along on a boat,
To sit in the sun or
To walk and search for
Pretty rocks.
This is Me!
I love to put my hair
In a ponytail and
Grab my tennis racket
For a casual game.
This is Me!
I love to dance,
I love to sing,
I love it in the Spring.

This is Me!
I love my children,
I love to kiss them
Goodnight,
I love nudging them
In the dawns early light.
This is Me!
Sometimes I sit outside
With my sketch pad
And draw something that
Inspires me ...
A tree, a rose, heaven knows?
This is Me!
I love to catch the
Wondering eye of a child;
Or sit and play with a few
Simple items.
Laughing, smiling, clapping, and singing.
This is Me!
I love God,
He inspires me every day.
When someone touches me ...
Or something inspires me ...
The words come rolling off the page.
Many times God is there
Laying out the words
Before I am aware.
This is Me!
I love to surprise someone
With a kindness;
I love to take notice
Of someone who is forgotten.
This is Me!
I love with all my heart,
I am there when someone
Needs help;
It uplifts me.
This is Me!

When my true love came
He was gentle and kind.
He wanted help with his family,
He was troubled.
I was there,
I helped. I cared.
When I was not acknowledged
I was hurt,
I was quiet,
I prayed.
His heart knows the way.
This is Me!
Don't tell me how to act
For you don't know my path.
Don't chastise or pass judgement on me
For you have not
Lived my life for me.
Don't look at me with disdain
For I have not driven
This train.
God is here,
He chose me,
He brought me on
This journey.
This is Me!

CHAPTER 2
God's Compassion

"Grandpa" is about my grandfather who was always so happy. There is a book in our family of his poetry. He wrote poetry for young men in the service to send to their loved ones. We used to visit our grandparents every weekend when I was little.

"I Remember Audrey"; Audrey was my older cousin from Canada. I attended her funeral. She died young. I remember how sweet and loving she was growing up. During times when I am struggling, I remember her and try to stand up strong.

"Knowledge" is about how we can learn all kinds of things in this world of information. But knowledge with the wisdom of God is a deeper, stronger knowledge in a world of appearances. As I have drawn closer to God he shapes and guides me in wisdom.

"The Dreamer" … God gave me this poem to encourage me and keep my hope alive. He helped me start writing again and painting my tiles. It is okay to dream big dreams.

"Rain from Heaven" is about how rain is cleansing and a blessing. When God sends down rain it is beautiful, gentle, and abundant.

> "Why standest there afar off, O Lord. Why hidest thou thyself in times of trouble?" (Psalms 10:1 KJV)

Grandpa

(Dedicated to Charles W. Phipps)
Grandpa, I remember you!
I remember how you
Always said hello to me
And were glad to see me
When I came to visit.
I remember the walks
Home from kindergarten;
I remember having orange soda and cheese popcorn
With you at the Knights of Columbus.
I remember how you would
Get so excited about the horse races.
Grandpa, I remember you!
You were funny and fun,
I remember the donuts and
The root beer floats.
I remember the Easter egg hunts
In your backyard.
Grandpa, I remember you!
Just sitting on the
Back swing,
Smoking a cigar.
I remember you always said, hi
And smiled at me.
Grandpa, I remember you.
Now I am a poet
Like you were.
That surprised me!
But it warms my heart
Grandpa, I remember you!

Hope

Today for the first time
In a long time
I feel hopeful.
Today God smiled and laughed
With me when I played
With a baby.
Today, God said, "Thank you"
To me
Because I helped a family
Understand how to help
Their child.
He said,
"That is why I picked you."
Today God touched my heart
And opened doors.
Today I was calm,
I felt hope.
I started thinking of
All that has happened,
But he has helped me
Have resolve.
Today I was hopeful
I could see things
I have been struggling with
More clearly.
Today
I
      Let
            Go!
I
      Let
            God
                  Lead
                      The
                         Way!
                             I have Hope!

I Remember Audrey

(Dedicated to Audrey)
Last night,
I could not sleep,
I could not cry,
I could not weep.
I was restless,
I was anxious,
I could not settle down.
I kept thinking about the truths
And how I yearned for justice.
God and the angels kept trying
To quiet my heart.
Then you came …
Audrey,
You came so sweetly
And compassionately,
That is just how
I remember you.
You know my walk,
Trying to recover from
All the abuse.
You tried to stand strong,
You were almost gone,
But a vile trick
Was played on you.
This ended your life.
I remember the funeral,
I remember those days.
They were full of
Heart-wrenching dismay.
My father was so brokenhearted,
He loved you so.
But, Audrey, I remember you,
You were always so sweet and kind,
You helped take care of us

When we came to visit.
The summer I stayed in
Your family's home
You were very gracious and caring.
I remember at night,
You knelt beside your bed and
Prayed;
Then you said, "goodnight."
You were so beautiful and lovely.
Audrey, I remember you.
You came to me last night
To reassure me
I am not lost,
You understand my
Hurt and pain.
Audrey, you tried to
Stand strong,
But your life was
Swept away.
I try to remember you
Whenever I need to stand strong,
And I always pray for God
To bring justice, today.

The Fountain of Life

Drink from the
Fountain of Life,
Look at your reflection
In the face of God,
Drink of love,
Drink of laughter,
Spread great joy
Amongst you.   ·
Cry out in the night
To your Savior,
He will rescue you
From your bindings;
He will carry you
On an adventure
Of a lifetime.
Drink of his blood
For he is the
Bread of life.
Drink of the love
Of Christ and
Thirst …
No more.

Knowledge

Knowledge is power,
But not all knowledge
Is truth.
Knowledge helps
Inform us
On the possibilities,
Knowledge feels good
Because it helps us grow,
Knowledge has endless bounds
It cannot be taken away,
Knowledge brings about
Truths,
But also can hide lies.
Knowledge is a tool
To help the learner
Become a bigger person,
Arising and growing in
Confidence.
Knowledge is a spiritual tool
But is most powerful
When God brings us to it.
Knowledge is the reality
That what appears to be
May not always be the truth.
Knowledge without
The love of God
Is limited,
But knowledge with
The wisdom of God
Knows no bounds.

The Dreamer

Believes in impossible dreams,
Hold tight to those dreams.
Inspires others to dream,
Gives many blessings through
Their positive attitude
In their conquest to achieve
Their dreams.
The dreamer is never dismayed
At the mountains in the way,
But perseveres by relying
On a higher power
To drive and direct them.
The dreamer,
Their heart knows the way,
They believe in what
They cannot see,
They persevere amongst great odds.
The dreamer loves everyone ... everywhere,
The dreamer loves to give
Because the dreamer
Knows how to receive
The best dreams,
Is through giving of their hearts
To others.
The Dreamer
Loves life,
Engages in friendships and
Risks everything.
The ultimate surprise,
The Dreamers dreams
Always come true.

Sounds from Heaven

Sounds from heaven
Up above,
Angels singing out
God's Love,
Sounds so sweetly,
Soft and pure.
Please bring more
So I can endure
Sounds from heaven.
Shout to me,
Are you listening
For my cry?
Please do not
Make me sigh.
Sounds from heaven
Up above
Angels singing
About so much love.
Peace and joy
Radiate from above,
They bring me
So much love.
Sounds from heaven
Up above,
Angels singing
Of God's love,
Follow me
To the light
And the love,
Lull me to
Sleep
With sounds from
Above.
Sounds from heaven
Up above
Angels singing,
Sweetly,
About God's
Eternal love.

Do You Hear Me?

Do you hear me?
Listen, please ...
For I have so
Many needs.
Can I have ...
... a car
... or boat?
Do you see
What's wrong
With my throat?
Wailing, whimpering ...
Sounds I cry
Do you hear me?
For I sigh ...
I need you
To come so quick,
For I am feeling
Very sick.
I need compassion
From above
Will you listen?
Do you hear me weep ...?
Sigh and sigh?
Can you feel
My pain inside?
Do you hear me?
In the night,
Crying desperately
For the sight
Of God's pure light.
Do you hear me?
... I am here
Settle down ...
My dear,
All is calm
In the light
Now go back
To sleep ...
Tonight.

Rain from Heaven

Rain from heaven
Fall on my face,
Not a trace
Of tears,
I have no
Fears.
Rain from heaven
Waters my spirit,
Drops drizzle down and
Dark clouds
Are all around.
Rain from heaven
Fall on me,
Wash my feet
Upon this seat.
Rain from heaven
Up above,
Rain down smiles
And lots of hugs.

CHAPTER 3
Acceptance

"My Little Niece" ... My niece Lauren is so beautiful! A natural beauty exudes from her heart. When we lost our home, I was separated from my children. I could not give the gifts I used to. I just sent her a card. She sent me a text message: "Thank You!" It touched my heart. She understood and showed her compassion.

"The Authors" ... I wrote about the different experiences I have had learning to be an author at a book signing. I published a book but didn't know much about the industry. It is a humbling experience.

"Forgiveness" ... I wrote this poem because for me to be healed, happy, and living closer to God, I must lay down my burdens and forgive everyone who has judged and hurt me, including my oppressor. It has been hard to do this. I have to forgive everyone, even those who meant great harm due to hatred that existed long before I was born.

"To Be a Woman" ...

God has taught me how he wants women to walk. To be a strong Christian woman isn't easy. What we interpret as strong is not what God means. We need to lean into God for strength.

"Hear the right, O Lord, attend onto my cry, give ear unto my prayer, that goeth not out of feigned lips. Let my sentence come forth from thy presence; let thine eyes behold the things that are equal." (Psalm 17:1–2)

Joyous

Joyous days are coming,
Believe,
They will come true.
No longer will you
Be so blue,
Joyous days are coming,
Believe,
And take heart.
No longer will you and
Your true love
Be so far apart.
Joyous days are coming,
Believe,
I picked you
To do many
Great things,
And to gift you
To sing.
Joyous days are coming,
Believe,
Everything will feel
So fine
You will not feel
Like you've been
Left behind.
Joyous days are coming,
Believe,
I love you,
I sheltered and guided you
With the angels and
Heavens glorious love.
Joyous days are coming,
Believe,
They have begun.
Joyous, joyous, joyous
Days for you,
I send them
From above.

My Little Niece

(Dedicated to Lauren Harris)
My little niece,
My little love,
You are so sweet.
God sent you
From above.
My little niece,
You touch my heart,
For you give
Lots of love.
My little niece,
Your eyes
Sparkle and shine,
You make me smile
In these hard times.
My little niece,
God sent you
From above
To spread
All kinds of love.
My little niece,
When I was
Hurting so …
You sent me
A message.
It was just
A small
Thank you,
But to me
It was a
Much needed
Hug.
My little niece,
You are growing up
In such a beautiful way.
My little niece,
You are loved
By your aunt
So far away.

The Authors

The authors all gathered
To tell their stories,
Which one is the best,
Which one will have
All the Glory.
The authors all gathered,
Each one wanted to shine,
They boasted and chimed,
Which one of their stories
Were so fine.
The authors all gathered,
They wanted to share
All their thoughts
And their glories,
All of them each
Chimed in.
The authors all gathered,
But one was so quiet,
So sublime.
They noticed and chattered,
They sold many books,
But one was very quiet,
No boasts of her book.
The authors all gathered
With friendly replies,
They shared their stories
And their hard times,
But one was very quiet,
She didn't have
Much to say,
Who was the
Quiet author
They would all say.
She is the one
Who was sent

From above,
To share the words
God needs to be heard,
She is the one
Who will rise
With humility and grace,
The authors all gathered
In this small place.

Forgiveness

God has taught me
A better way to forgive,
A way that I can stand strong
And not be taken
Advantage of.
I have been hurt deeply
By many others,
He has been helping me
To guard my heart and
Stand strong.
He knows of the
Injustices,
But most of their lives
Have moved on.
He walks me out of
The ashes today,
He asks me to
Lay down the
Hurt and pain
I have accumulated
Over many years,
He asks me to forgive
Let go …
And love.
It has been hard,
For I trust only
In him,
He tells me it's okay,
I am safe now.
He is justifying me
From all the wrongs.
It's time to
Let go
And live again.
Today I have forgiven

All those who have
Hurt me and my family.
Today I am at
Peace,
He is here,
He is holding me
Tightly,
He is justifying me.
Today I have
Forgiven.

My Savior

My Savior walks quietly
Along the seashore,
Listening to the waves
And the sea gulls.
My Savior walks quietly,
His sandals touch the shore,
He is listening to his
Father above,
He walks with his hands
Full of great things to do.
He isn't worried,
He is calm,
He does not rush
For he wants to see
The beauty around him.
He walks quietly and patiently,
Each step with such grace.
He picks up the weary, hungry
And those who have been
Forgotten.
He walks with them
Quietly
Healing their hearts.
He has a large to do list,
He doesn't feel distraught,
He walks with the
Angels and Saints,
He gives glory to
God above
For he is a peaceful man
Full of love.
My Savior walks quietly
Along the seashore,
Taking time with his Father
And praying for those
Who are no more.

To Be a Woman

What it means
To be a woman,
You have to be
Very strong
Because life
Isn't fair.
You have to know
You are beautiful
Beyond compare.
No matter what
The world may say
Or think about you,
You have to know
God put you here
To nurture and love
Others.
He gave you deep
Compassion
And asks you to
Share it with others.
You have to be
Strong in him
So he can carry you
Through the heartaches
In life.
Remember,
He will always
Be with you.
To be a woman
In the world today
Means you are a
Guardian of virtue
And fidelity
Against a world
That wants you to

Let go of those
Values.
A woman smiles and shines
From within outward,
Even when her world
Is falling apart
She stands strong
Because God is
Holding her up.
He reveres the women
In the world
Because they protect
The future of the world.
To be a woman means
Humility, love, joy and
Laughter,
It means to be wise,
Listen more often
Than you speak
So that others will
Listen when you speak.
To be a woman
Of God
Means you are not
Perfect
In the eyes of the world
But in the eyes
Of God
He is your only
Judge
His love for you is …
Never ending.

Sitting Here in the Quiet

Sitting here in the quiet
Knowing you are here
To catch me when
I stumble and fall,
Sitting here in the quiet
With you holding my hand
Renders a security
I do not understand,
Sitting here in the quiet
Where I am
Nurtured and loved
Keeps me calm,
Helps me see hope
When I am
In your arms.
Sitting here in the quiet
Waiting for my
True love to come,
My Father sits
Teaching me and
Showing me the things
To come.
Sitting here in the quiet
I know all that
I've done
Is not in vain
And the truth
Will come.
Sitting here in the quiet
In God's holy place
There is no
Destruction,
There is only
Grace.

Acceptance

Today I am quiet.
I feel balanced,
As if someone is
Holding me tight;
I'm not struggling
With anxiety and fear,
Just quiet, calm.
I'm writing poetry
And talking with God,
I have questions
But I feel satisfied,
Content.
The past seems to be
Over now,
I'm not churning
The reruns,
Just quiet.
An acceptance that
What is … is …,
But the tides are
Turning,
New life and hopeful
Tomorrows fill my
Spirit.
I'm calm, content.
I feel loved,
God has brought me
Through the storm …
Acceptance.

CHAPTER 4
Trusting in God

"When will they come?" …

Now that God has revealed the truths and justified me, I wondered: When will the people who I felt were close to me come into my life again with true hearts, not pretending? I wrote this poem asking God … When will they come?

"Truths and Trust"

These poems are about how God reveals the truths in our lives. It is not just about those who have betrayed us, but about ourselves. So that he can shape and refine us. Trust is just that. How to trust again after a dark storm that has left us alone.

"The Trial"

After my children's father died, we gathered for small group at my home. It was a large group that gathered that day. They questioned me about the death and funeral. We previously attended a very rich church and were actively involved as a family. Many people attended the funeral. After that they judged and shunned me. I refer to that small group as "The Trial."

"Deliver me from mine enemies, O my God: defend me from them that rise up against me. Deliver me from the workers of iniquity, and save me from bloody men. For, lo, they lie in wait for my soul: the mighty are gathered against me; not for my transgressions, nor for my sin, O Lord." (Psalm 59:1–3)

When will they come?

I'm quiet,
The storm is over.
But now, I ask God
When will they come?
The family members
Who chastised me,
When will they come?
The people I befriended
Who I am learning to
Trust again,
When will they come?
The adventures and wonders,
When will they come?
The rainbows and God's
Promises,
When will they come?
The times of endless
Joy,
When will he come?
My true love.
God quiets my spirit
Wraps me in His love
Someday, my child …
Someday soon.

Solemn

When things are quiet,
When you can't hear
A thing,
The solemnness
Can bring great things.
When the night is
Peaceful,
Like on a cool, crisp evening,
The solemn is there.
As you look up at the
Bright lights,
Solemn is good,
It helps refresh our
Perspective.
We lay down our
Baggage,
Everything feels light,
Solemn is good.
It rests our busy lives,
It quiets our thoughts
Into the night.
As sleep takes hold
And the sounds of Angels
Can be heard,
Solemnness
Brings rest
And refreshes our
Souls.

I was there ...

In the night
When my children
Were crying ...
I was there
In the daytime
When there were
Things to be done ...
I was there
In the evening
When there was
Homework to be done ...
I was there
When the children were
Being photographed ...
I was there
When they were
Confused and had questions ...
I was there
When it was dinner time
And a meal had to be prepared ...
I was there
When my children
Had to be picked up from school ...
I was there
When it was time
To go to practice ...
I was there
When they needed school supplies ...
I was there
When our world was
Falling apart and my children
Were being victimized ...
I was there
When they wanted me to know
How scared and confused

They were …
I was there
When they had
Special events or
Needed uniforms …
I was there …
Where were you?

Truths

Sometimes truths are
Hard to bear,
They reveal lies and
Deceptions
That are right in front of us.
We are disheartened and
Discouraged by what
God reveals to us.
He holds us tight,
He wants us to stand strong,
He will fight the fight.
Sometimes truths show us
Our close friends
Are imposters
Out for their own gain.
Sometimes truths show
Humility,
A hard lesson to learn
In a world of boastfulness.
Sometimes truths show us
Our family members are
Not supporting us
Even though we have
Supported them.
A very heart-wrenching
Truth.
Sometimes truth shows us
A betrayal of the most
Personal nature,
A very difficult truth
To face.
It can bring us
To our knees,
But God walks in
And helps us to

Stand up again.
He shows deep
Love and compassion,
He helps us live again,
Trust again,
And begin a new way
Of life.
Sometimes
Truths
     Can
          Make
               You
                    Feel
                        All
                             Alone …

But Jesus
Walks this world
To help those who are
Abandoned and alone.
The best truth to
Always remember is
Jesus
You are never alone
Jesus is love!

So Many Days

So many days,
So many tears,
So many doubts,
So many fears.
Feelings of loss,
Disappointment and shame,
They hold you hostage
From words of Great Fame.
So many promises
I have yet to keep.
So, my daughter,
Why do you weep?
The sun was shining
Outside today,
Inviting you to come out
And play,
But you sat in a corner
With hurt and dismay.
My daughter … why?
Why didn't you
Come out and play?
So much worry,
So much furry.
Lay down your anger,
Your Father is here.
So, my daughter,
The days are getting longer
For Spring is almost here.
Please lay down
All the past
For the future you dreamed about
Is near.
Your Father and the Angels
Have come very close,
They want you to know

That the tears
Will disappear
And the bluebirds and rainbows
Will soon be here.
The past is over,
Lay down your sword,
You have fought a
Mighty battle.
God has been your
Protector,
Your armor and shield,
Now enjoy the beauty
That surrounds you,
For now
Peace is here.

Trust

I know, my daughter,
You have been hurt
And betrayed by a
Vicious conspiracy.
The hatred and vile plans
That surrounded you
For many years
Were taken note of
By God above.
He will redeem
Your honor
And raise you
Higher than promised,
For you followed him
Above all else,
Your eyes were on the
Lord.
Trust is difficult in
A world where everything
Is not as it seems.
You will walk
Stronger now,
I will always
Protect you,
Just like I did when
You were unaware of the
Evil that surrounded you.
Trust is not easy
When you have had
Such betrayal
In your life,
Even from those
Close to your heart.
Trust, my daughter,
Is freeing,

Lay down the trouble
Of the past,
You are walking closer
To me.
After enduring
Such trials
You can trust in
Your children and
Your true love.
If you have doubts
Or fears
Bring them to me,
Trust in your Savior,
I am the Alpha and the Omega,
Justice comes through me.
Everything comes
To justice in the end
For God wants all
Hearts to be filled with
The love he has created
For you to experience.
So, my daughter,
Celebrate Life,
Enjoy the good times,
Lean into me for
Understanding
And when the clouds come
I am in the rain,
I am carrying you
Through
Ending all the
Strife,
Believe and trust
In me!

Beauty

(song)
Beauty beneath me,
Beauty above me,
Beauty inside me,
Astounds and guides me.
Beauty so deeply
My emotions subside
As glassy tears
Run down from
My eyes.
Beauty so everlasting,
Beauty so motionless
And timeless,
Beauty subsides
Through my eyes,
Beauty astounds me,
Beauty is all around me,
Beauty of God and
His elegant angels,
Beauty so purely
Delivered so compassionately.
Beauty beneath me,
Beauty above me,
Beauty inside me,
Astounds and guides me.
Beauty so simply,
Beauty so plainly
In front of me
And beside me,
Beauty wraps its love
Around me.
Romantic and humbly
It seeps deep inside me,
Beauty surrounds me,
Beauty exudes me,

Beauty from my God
So humbly enthroned
From above.
Beauty beneath me,
Beauty above me,
Beauty inside me,
So humbly he
Guides me
Assuring my past,
Clearing away all
Of the rath.
Beauty so purely
It simply endures me,
Beauty from God,
The purest
Love of all.
He simply adores me,
Nurtures and secures me
For the journey
He leads me on
Straight from above.
Beauty beneath me,
Beauty above me,
Beauty inside me,
So pure is
His love.

The Trial

They all came to small group
One day after the funeral.
My children's father died,
There was a big funeral.
Afterwards you gathered
In my home,
For small group,
You came in numbers.
The leader asked me
To explain what happened,
I was hesitant to speak.
Everyone saw a big, rich church
Full of people
But you asked your questions.
I answered the best I could,
I didn't know all the
Truths
But I did love him.
You all judged me.
After that small group
Only a few people came,
Every time
Mostly gawkers
Who came to see
What the gossip
Was all about.
Soon less and less
People came.
I thought maybe my house
Wasn't clean enough,
Maybe I should make
Different foods.
None of this worked,
Then God showed me.
When my best friend

Who I hadn't seen
Since I bought this home,
She came to observe
The gossip,
She believed and came
As an imposter,
My best friend
Since childhood.
God kept revealing
The imposters,
He showed me
Church leaders who
Came to see me.
The spectacle
WOW!
Soon no one came.
The house was clean,
Food was made,
Candles were lit,
But no one came.
God revealed,
My Pastor ran out of
People to send.
I continued to prepare,
Hoping someone would
Come to my small group.
No one came
Then …
We lost our home.
The trial was complete,
The sentence guilty,
The punishment,
The loss of our home,
And the separation
Of our family.
The trial.

A Letter to the Church

I met you on a
Mission Trip,
I only saw all
Of the good you
Were doing.
Everyone was working hard
To help the families
Rebuild from
Hurricane Katrina.
I noticed how quiet and
Humble everyone was.
I met a couple of
Young women and
Became friends with them.
When you gathered
To play volleyball
On the beach
Everyone just got along,
Everyone was included.
It was beautiful,
Fellowship.
We sat on the beach
At sunset for prayer,
I loved meeting
All of you,
I know God
Wanted me here.
On our way home
It was quiet.
Everyone was tired
From all the work.
I thought this was
The kind of church
I wanted my children
To be a part of ...

I met you …
Each one …
Serving God
But
The days and months
To come,
I met the truths.
They weren't so
Pleasant …
If only you could
Have seen
What I did
On that mission trip.
It was the best of you
On the beach
At sunset
In Lakeshore, Mississippi,
I saw a church.

CHAPTER 5
God Leads the Way

"Leading" is about God's definition of leading. He keeps bringing me to it. He pushes me out front. He won't let me falter. He shapes me and teaches me. Leading is not about manipulating and controlling everything.

"My Flowers" …

I gave a gift of two planter flowers to my true love and his mother. But part of what ended our relationship was that I noticed he put them on his back porch, and they were dying. After that day, I left. I had to decide what I wanted in my life. He planted those flowers in front of his house. Every year he plants flowers there for me. I know I am in his heart. Last year, the flowers were one of my favorite colors, pink.

"Things Are Different Now" …

This poem I wrote when I moved into my new home with my children. Our home was calm and peaceful. I felt very free and loving. I no longer made choices with indecision. I knew what I wanted.

"Sister" …

I dedicated to a single Mother with two special-needs children. I met her as a young teacher with her first child. I met her again many years later with her second child. I wanted her to know she is a beautiful mother, despite her struggles.

"I will hear what God the Lord will speak: for he will speak peace unto his people, and to his saints: but not let them turn again to folly." (Psalm 85:8)

Leading

Leading is about walking alone,
Standing up for
What you believe in,
No matter what
Others think.
Leading is following
A vision,
Not of what is
But of what could be.
Following your heart,
Knowing what is
Right and just.
No one to hide behind,
You are out there
Wrapped with the armor
Of God's love and grace.
Leading brings forth change
And requires
Steadfast perseverance,
Trusting in God
To guide you
As you step out
Front to lead.
Leading strengthens your
Character
And brings about
Great Things.
Leading is stepping out
And walking the path
You are meant to walk.
Leading is what
God
Chose for you.
Step out in
Trust and faith,
He will do
The rest.

Close To You

I feel close to you,
In the quiet
Amongst the wind
And the blue sky,
A peace has come
Over me,
Unlike anything I have
Ever felt before.
Close to you
I feel the comfort
Of your love
Wrapped around me,
Close to you
There is no fear,
Only promises
Hope and joy.
Close to you
I dream impossible
Dreams,
I awake and
Watch them
Unfold before my eyes.
Close to you
I tremble
When you show me
Your enormous strength
And your compassionate
Love for me.
Close to you
Is where I want to be
The rest of my days.
No burdens, no weight,
You carry them all,
Close to you
You read my heart

And show me
How to be true
To what you created.
Me to be
Close to you,
Oh Lord,
Is the only place
I want to be …

Fruits of the Spirit

Fruits of the Spirit
Help us balance
Our lives,
They give us strength
And a sense of
Centeredness.
Fruits of the Spirit
Are simple ways
We can keep our lives
Aligned in the
Spirit of God.
Fruits of the Spirit
Help us to listen
In the quiet
For God's guidance.
Fruits of the Spirit
Are the keys to
Joy, peace and love.
Walk strong in the
Light and love,
The fruits of the spirit
Will bring you
Closer to me
I am here!

Simplify Your Lives

All the hustle and bustle,
No time for anything.
Zooming here and there,
Everyone is going so fast.
They forget to stop and rest,
Just on a race
To nowhere,
Collecting things along
The way.
They have
Only to reflect on
Their lives and are overwhelmed
With the clutter
They need to organize.
I tell you, children,
You do not need
All those things.
Simplify your lives,
Enjoy simple things
Again,
I put them here.
Listen to the songs
Of the birds and animals,
I put here for you.
Take a walk with me
And look around
At the trees, plants, and flowers
I put here
For you to enjoy.
Simplify your lives,
Children,
Just turn around,
Look up to the sky,
Enjoy the paintings
Created across the sky,

Enjoy the warmth
Of the sunshine,
And the gentle touch
Of the warm summer
Breezes.
Simplify your lives,
Children,
For it is in the
Simple things
I gave you
That will bring you
Happiness
In your lives.

The Window of Life

The window of life
I can see through
Displays the beauty
Of the world
For all to see.
The window of life
Shows beautiful babies
And young toddlers
Playing in the sunshine.
The window of life
Sees through the
Teenage years
Of becoming your
Own special you.
The window of life
Clearly defines
Your heart
And reflects the
Love within it.
The window of life
Peeks through your adulthood
And into old age.
The window of life
Ages with time
And becomes
Wiser.
The window of life
Pulls the shade
And the light goes out.
But the window of life
Is just the beginning
Of an Eternal Life
With me.
The window of life
Lets in the

Warm gentle breezes,
The chirping of young
Baby birds,
And the warmth of
The sunshine.
The window of life
May seem
Fleeting
But it is just
The beginning
Of all that I have
Promised.

My Flowers

(Dedicated to My True Love Ernie Hill)
There they are,
So beautiful,
Sitting in front
Of your house—
Pink.
My flowers adorn
Your house,
I am in your heart
But you are not ready
To release your secret;
You keep our love
Locked in your heart,
No one can touch it,
No one can see,
But I can see
How much you love me.
My pink flowers
On your porch,
Showing that you
Still love me.
But I need
More than
Flowers,
I need you
Standing strong
Claiming our love
In the sunlight,
My pink flowers
A symbol of our love
For one another.
I see them,
My heart hurts.
I need you to
Claim it
In the sunlight,
My flowers,
Our love.

His Majesty

God has taken me
On a tour of his
Majestic Mountains,
He has shown me
His glorious works.
Whether barren or lush,
The overwhelming feeling
Of something so majestic,
Created by God,
Just to climb
One of his mountains
Humbles my soul,
Something so grand
Towering over all the land.
A majestic mountain,
High above the land and water,
To sit up there
So high
And look out at his
Wondrous works
Brings peace
To my soul.
His Majesty,
Laid out throughout
The world
Peacefully stands
Overlooking the land,
Showing how mighty
Our Savior is,
His Majesty.

Things Are Different Now

Now I wake up to the
Sunshine and God's love.
No longer do I wake up
With a list in my head
And holding my breath.
Now I take a walk
With God every morning,
No longer waiting for
The griping and complaining.
Now I cook a meal
And everyone is satisfied,
No longer am I evaluated
And put down at the
Start of the day.
Now I smile and laugh
When something is
Funny or feels good,
No longer feeling numb
And helpless.
Now I know
What I want,
No longer do I think
I am not worthy
Of something,
Now everyone cares and loves
One another,
Giving hugs and kisses freely,
No longer hiding until
The storm is over.
Now God leads my life,
Now I feel beautiful,
Now I feel loved,
Now there are no worries,
Because I pass them
Onto God.

Sister

I see a single mom
With an overwhelming
Burden,
I see a beautiful
Heart
Warm, caring and loving.
In solitude, spending
Time with our Lord,
I see a spiritual
Woman
Reaching out to others,
Nurturing her children,
Kindness, gentleness, and patience.
I see a sister of God
With many worries,
Never complaining.
I see a beautiful
Woman
Living out a life
For God.
I pray
Many blessings
Come her way.

Sweetness

The succulent smell of a rose,
The beauty of redemption,
Sweetness.
The Glory of God,
When He lifts you high
Above the mountains,
Sweetness.
The inspirational feeling
Deep in your heart,
Where he wraps you
In His Love,
Sweetness.
The glory of a new day
Beginning
As the sun rises
Over the horizon,
Sweetness.
Sitting in the quiet
Watching a newborn sleeping
And then slowly
Awakening,
Sweetness.
The tender touch of
A mother's soft kiss
On her baby's forehead,
Sweetness.
Gentle tuck-ins,
Warm goodbyes,
Welcoming hugs,
Sweetness.

CHAPTER 6
Something for God to Do

"Something for God to Do" I wrote when I was learning to let go. I stopped trying to save the day and carrying everything. Some things are only for God to do. He is very strong. We don't have to carry the burdens.

"A Beacon in the Night" is about my true love. We talked about how God is leading our lives. His lifestyle, I know he wanted to change because he was drawn to me. I was clear I was a Christian and that God was leading my life. God keeps bringing him and I together for brief encounters. Each time he reveals how he has changed and turned his life to walk closer to God. We are each beacons for each other. The way we walk with God draws others who do not know God or have lost their way to draw closer to him.

"Whispers"

God gave me this poem. It is one of my favorites. It is about how loving and nurturing God is when he is taking care of us and guiding us when we are broken and alone. My cup runneth over.

"The Shepherd"

God gave me this poem to reassure me I am safe. He is always near, to lean into him when I am confused or fearful. He is steady. He will never leave me.

"As for me, I will behold thy face in righteousness: I shall be satisfied, when I awake, with thy likeness." (Psalm 17:15, KJV)

Something For God to Do ...

I am worried about
The future for my children.
I close my eyes,
Open my heart,
And ask God to add
This to his list.
He puts it in his
Something for God to-do box.
I am sleeping,
I toss and turn,
I awake suddenly,
I fear I forgot
To tell someone
I love him.
I pray and ask God
To watch over him.
God puts it in his
Something for God to-do box.
I am driving
Down the freeway,
I hear a noise
Coming from the engine,
My heart begins to beat fast,
I worry something
Is very wrong.
I pray for God
To help me find out
What is wrong.
God takes it and
Puts it in his
Something for God to-do box.
Suddenly
I begin to laugh more,
I am happy more
Than sad.

Slowly,
In his own time,
He answers all
Of those requests
In his God box.
He reveals the answers
Gently and perfectly,
In his own time.
My load gets lighter,
Something about me is
Glowing,
These things aren't for me
To fix.
I smile and love
And God takes care
Of the requests
In his
Something for God to-do box.

You Are Beautiful

(song)
You are beautiful,
So beautiful
To me,
You are beautiful,
So beautiful
To me.
When the sun
Shines on your face
I can feel
Your grace,
You are beautiful,
So beautiful
To me.
You are beautiful,
So beautiful
To me,
I can feel
Your warm embrace
As you touch
My face.
You are beautiful,
So beautiful
To me,
You are beautiful,
So beautiful
To me.
When your heart
Is shining bright
You light up
The night,
You are beautiful,
So beautiful
To me.
You are beautiful,

So beautiful
To me.
When you walk with me
And show me
All you see,
You are beautiful,
So beautiful
To me.
You are beautiful,
So beautiful
To me,
I can imagine
All that can be
When you walk
Close to me.
You are beautiful,
So beautiful
To me,
When I am down
Upon one knee
Praying for you
To comfort me.
You are beautiful,
So beautiful
To me,
You're always
At my side
You will never
Hide.
You are beautiful,
So beautiful
To me,
As you walk me to
Your heavenly place
I feel the warmth
Of your grace.
You are beautiful,
So beautiful to me,

When I reach
My resting place
I'll feel your
Warm embrace.
You are beautiful,
So beautiful
To me.

Whispers

Whispers in the wind,
I love you,
My child.
Whispers in my ear
As I gently
Drift off to sleep,
Rest, my child,
I am your
Comforter
Fear not.
Whispers in the morning,
I am here,
My child,
I will always be near.
Whispers in my trials,
I am carrying you,
My child,
Lean into me.
Whispers in my heart,
You will do
Great things,
My child,
I will walk you
To the Promised Land.
Whispers of my Father's
Eternal love for me.

A Beacon in the Night

I am a beacon in the night,
Someone is following me,
I am following Jesus,
He tells me remain silent.
I am a beacon for someone
Who has lost their way,
They look to me
To change,
I am following Jesus …
My beacon.
He tells me I am a beacon
For someone who does not
Know the way out.
Jesus walks before me,
He takes his time to
Teach me his ways,
For someone is watching me.
They are lost!
They are alone!
They look to me for guidance,
I am their beacon in the night.
Jesus is my beacon,
A beacon in the night!

By God's Design

You are created
In the image of God.
He sculpts and molds you
To a perfect design,
No two are the same,
Each heart filled
With gifts and hidden treasures.
You are formed
By God's design,
Molded into his image,
Given grace and mercy
To grow and flourish,
Blessing the world,
With the love
That he gave you.
You are created
By God's personal design,
You are not
Weird or an outcast,
You were purposefully and
Wonderfully made
By God's design,
Nurtured and loved.
He never leaves
Your side
For He created you
For a special purpose,
To bless others
With love.
You are created
By God's design,
His love for you
Runs deep
With crimson blood,
He gave his life

So you may live
To flourish and create,
To love and be loved.
Hold onto the blessings
God has written on
Your heart,
You are nurtured and loved
By the Great Creator,
No design exactly the same.
So love and be loved,
Laugh and spread laughter,
Let great joy fill your heart,
Let peace and tranquility
Be at the end
Of each day,
For you are created
By God's design,
An eternal love
That can never fail.
You are uniquely created
By God's design.

Together

(song)
Together we learn,
Together we fly,
Together we reach,
To soar above the sky.
Together we hope,
Together we pray,
Together we learn,
To walk in His own way.
Together we dream,
Together we hope,
A new day will come
For others to pray
And learn God's
Everlasting ways.
Together we soar,
Amongst the blue skies,
To see what blessings
God has on the other side.
Together we dream,
Together we strive,
To know that God
Is bringing a big surprise.
So, lighten your load,
Lean only onto Him,
For He knows the way
To bring joy and praise
To His name.
Your heart will be filled
with unending joy,
So lay down your load,
He can show you the way.
Together we learn,
Together we strive,
For God to teach us

His dream for our lives.
So, open your heart,
Bring love to the world,
And the one who loves you
Will bring great joy
To many lives.

The Love in Your Heart

I see the love in your heart,
No one knows it like me,
It is warm and everlasting,
Full of dreams and
The deepest depths.
I see the love in your heart,
No one sees what I see,
Beautiful, heartwarming hugs
And deep disappointments.
I see the love in your heart,
No one feels it like me,
In the wounds of my
Hands and my feet
As you strive to be
Accepted in this strange world.
I see the love in your heart,
No one comforts it like me,
As you stumble and fall
And stand up again,
Trying to be a warrior
In my name.
I see the love in your heart,
No one loves it like me,
I love the prayers and thanksgivings
As you hope for others,
I love the endurance and giving
As you lend a helping hand.
I see the love in your heart,
No one knows it like me,
As you walk in this life
Following me,
Your compassion for others and
Me,
As you walk with me
To eternity,

Yes,
I see the love in your heart,
No
    One
        Knows
            It
                Like
                    Me!

Ask Me for What You Want

Ask me for what you want,
Do not be afraid.
Ask me! My child,
What is it that you
Want today?
Do you want to be happy?
Do you want to be loved?
For, my child, all you need to do
Is ask,
For you are truly loved.
The Father wants to bestow on you
Many blessings from above,
So just
Ask me, child.
Ask me,
Do not be afraid,
Ask me for what you want,
I'll grant it right away.

The Shepherd

I am your shepherd,
You are my sheep,
Follow closely.
Stay with your shepherd,
For vile things and
Cruel deeds
Walk amongst you,
I can protect you
And make giants fall,
Their lives will not
Prosper.
Yours will be filled with
The fruits of the spirit,
So, try to stay close
To your shepherd.
For I am wise
Beyond your years,
I have walked this land,
Only I know the way,
I am your shepherd,
Stay close to me, children.

CHAPTER 7
Salvation

As I have been healing from the pain and the heartaches, at times, I needed to understand everything. "Frozen Hearts" is about how people judged me and my children after the death of their father. They didn't live the truths we did. They didn't know the truths. Their gossip spread like wildfire and hurt me and my children.

"I Never Asked" ...

My true love approached me for help and friendship at work. He was not a stranger. I worked with him for many years. He walked into my classroom one day and saw my husband being mean to me.

"The Simple Things" ...

God gave me this poem to let me know it isn't in how much we have or how big a party we throw or how many gifts we give. It's about our interactions with each other. The Simple Things are the memories we keep. They are precious.

"Great is the Lord, and greatly to be praised in the city of our God, in the mountain of his holiness." (Psalm 48:1)

Frozen Hearts

You are beautiful,
You are loved eternally,
Your heart is not frozen,
You have experienced
The frozen hearts of others
Who have believed in
Gossip from hatred,
Strewn from jealousy.
Frozen hearts turn
Their backs on others,
They don't lend a helping hand,
Frozen hearts bring darkness
Instead of light,
Frozen hearts throw
Icicles and frigid stares.
They don't bring warmth,
They don't show that
They care.
Frozen hearts throw snowballs and
Winds of blizzards
Where they go,
They don't stop everything
To bring aid to ones they care,
Frozen hearts tear down bridges
And cry they don't care,
For their eyes are cold to the
Ones that stare.
Frozen hearts hurt and
Throw their rules around,
They lash out with opinions
That others have spawned,
Frozen hearts don't care
That the truth is not fair.
Frozen hearts,
They bring pain,

They bring suffering,
They don't build up,
They tear down.
Frozen hearts can be found
Almost everywhere.
Beware,
They are strong and fierce
But they don't care.
They are right,
They build themselves up,
With boastful airs.
Frozen hearts,
They build walls,
They leave
A chill in the air,
Frozen hearts
They are everywhere.
Frozen hearts
Don't stop and stare,
Frozen hearts
Freeze the bitter air,
So, if you feel
A brisk chill in the air.
A frozen heart
May be near
So, you better …
                    BEWARE!

Sleep

Tonight, I can't sleep,
I can't stop thinking
Of all the fears,
I am trying to sleep
But I can't count sheep,
Instead, I am spinning
The day's events in my head.
I am worried and fearful,
I toss and turn,
I pray for God's guidance,
I pray for peace,
I pray for love,
But I can't sleep.
I toss and turn,
I cry out to God to bring
His angels and send me
Off to sleep.
My anxious body
Is overcome with a quietness,
The anxiety stops,
I feel loved and held.
I become very calm,
I feel God's love
Overtake me,
And I fall off
To sleep …

Beauty

Beauty comes from
Within,
Beauty glows when
Your heart is full,
Beauty isn't
Ribbons and bows,
Beauty is refined
In your character.
When God touches you
Beauty flows from your heart.

I Never Asked

I never asked you to hold
My hand,
You asked me to hold
Your hand.
I never asked you to
Kiss me,
You asked me to
Kiss you.
I never asked you to
Look into my deep blue eyes,
You asked me to
Look into your deep brown eyes.
I never asked you
For help,
You asked me
For help.
When your father was dying
I never asked you
To love me,
I just opened
My heart to you.
You asked me to
Love you,
But I had already
Fallen in love with you.
I never asked
You to pray for me,
You asked me to
Pray for you,
But I already have
And I never stopped.
I never asked you to say
"I Love You,"
You just said it,
On your knees,

So passionately.
I opened my heart
And expressed my love,
I took a big chance
On love,
After much pain and sorrow
I loved again,
I can't take back
My love,
For when I love
It is with all my heart.
You didn't stand up for me,
I stood up for you,
For my love for you
Knows no bounds.
You can't stand it
When I don't look at you,
It's written all over your face.
You blush when you see me,
But now,
I haven't seen you
In so ... ... long,
My heart is hurting
Because I can't stop
Loving you,
And I'm still waiting
For you to stand up
For me and tell the world
I am your true love.
For now, I am quiet,
I bring my hurt to Jesus
And I pray for my
True love
To claim his love ...
Someday ...

The Simple Things

The simple things
Bring you joy and laughter.
Please believe me
When I say,
The joyous times
Are the simplest times.
We need to sit and pray,
I love you
When you laugh,
Enjoy this life,
Believe.
The simple times
Are the best times.
Don't forget to play,
Be happy,
Love and be loved,
Relax.
Don't worry your
Life away,
The simple things
In life
Bring the best
Memories …
That please me
Each day.
The simple things
Touch your heart and
Joy and laughter
Are on display,
Believe.
I have much
For you to do
But don't
Complicate things.
Please pray …

The simplest things
Give you the deepest
Love.
Please pray ...
The simplest things
You see today
Will be the memories
You keep
So ...
Please pray ...
Enjoy the simple things
Of this life!

Give Thanks to God Above

Thank you, God,
For blessing me so,
Thank you for the
Flowers and the
Red, red rose.
Thank you for my
Daughter,
Her love is so pure.
Thank you for my
Son,
He is growing closer
To you.
Thank you for
Saving us
From great harm,
For guiding and protecting us
From those who
Meant harm.
Thank you for the
Love you taught us,
It keeps us as one.
Our family is closer,
For you are the one
Who guided and shielded us
From the storm,
Thank you, Father.

Thank you.

For now we are
Together and whole again.
We understand that love
Cannot be bought or sold,
The things that are stored
Heaven knows
They are not as important
As our love
For one another.
Thank you, Father,
For bringing warm hearts
To help us through
The storm.
Thank you, Father,
Thank you,
For now we have grown,
We are a family now …
People know the things
That you gave us
Were gifts from above
You provided for us,
But we cherish them
No more
Our love for each other
Is all the Gold we need.
You provided the shelter and
Protection in the storm.
Thank you, Father,
Thank you
For our lives and being
Born.

Printed in the United States
by Baker & Taylor Publisher Services